DIGGING UP THE PAST

THE CAVE OF ALTAMIRA

BY EMILY ROSE OACHS

BELLWETHER MEDIA • MINNEAPOLIS, MN

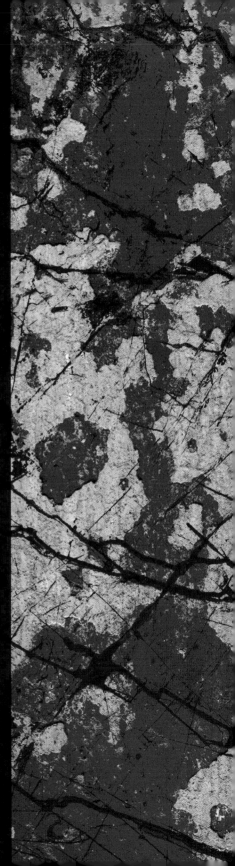

™

Are you ready to take it to the extreme? Torque books thrust you into the action-packed world of sports, vehicles, mystery, and adventure. These books may include dirt, smoke, fire, and chilling tales. **WARNING**: read at your own risk.

Library of Congress Cataloging-in-Publication Data

LC record for The Cave of Altamira available at
    https://lccn.loc.gov/2018061012

Editor: Betsy Rathburn   Designer: Brittany McIntosh

Printed in the United States of America, North Mankato, MN.

TABLE OF CONTENTS

A PREHISTORIC GALLERY

Cave walls surround you. You look up at the low ceiling. Rich colors stand out against the golden rock. You spot bison, deer, handprints, and **symbols**.

You are standing in a **replica** of the Cave of Altamira. During the last **Ice Age**, the real cave was filled with beautiful art.

CAVE ART

There are Ice Age cave paintings around the world. Among the most famous of these caves are Lascaux and Chauvet in France.

WHAT IS THE CAVE OF ALTAMIRA?

The Cave of Altamira is in northern Spain. It holds some of the earliest **Paleolithic** cave art ever discovered!

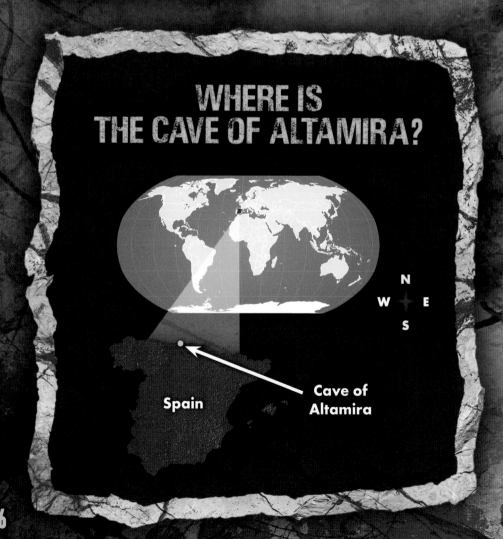

WHERE IS THE CAVE OF ALTAMIRA?

N
W E
S

Spain

Cave of Altamira

The cave is 971 feet (296 meters) long. Colorful paintings and **engravings** fill its length. They decorate the cave's walls and ceilings. Experts **estimate** the oldest might be at least 22,000 years old!

prehistoric
humans

Groups of **prehistoric** humans once lived
near Altamira. Experts believe the first moved
there about 36,000 years ago. People added
artwork to the cave over thousands of years.

WORLD OF COLOR

Much of Altamira's artwork is very detailed. It is also famous for its use of two or more colors!

Horses, wild oxen, and other large animals were common subjects. There were also unfamiliar symbols and some human hands.

Artists likely finished the last picture about 13,000 years ago. Years later, the entrance **collapsed** and sealed the cave shut.

Today's experts do not know the exact meaning of the artwork. Some think it was linked to religion or hunting. But all experts believe the art meant something to those who created it.

CAVE OF ALTAMIRA TIMELINE

about 36,000 years ago:
The first prehistoric humans move into the cave

about 13,000 years ago:
Artists create the last pictures in the cave

about 22,000 years ago:
Prehistoric humans create the first art in the cave

about 13,000 years ago:
The entrance to the cave collapses

REALISTIC PICTURES

The cave's walls and ceiling were full of bumps. Artists often used the rock's shape in their pictures. This made their figures look more lifelike.

1879:
A Spanish nobleman and his daughter discover the cave's paintings

2001:
An exact replica of the cave opens to the public

1868 CE:
A hunter finds the cave

1985:
The Cave of Altamira becomes protected by UNESCO

A DISCOVERY
THAT CHANGED HISTORY

**Marcelino
Sanz de Sautuola**

The Cave of Altamira sat untouched
for 13,000 years. In 1868, a hunter found
the cave. He told local **nobleman**
Marcelino Sanz de Sautuola about it.

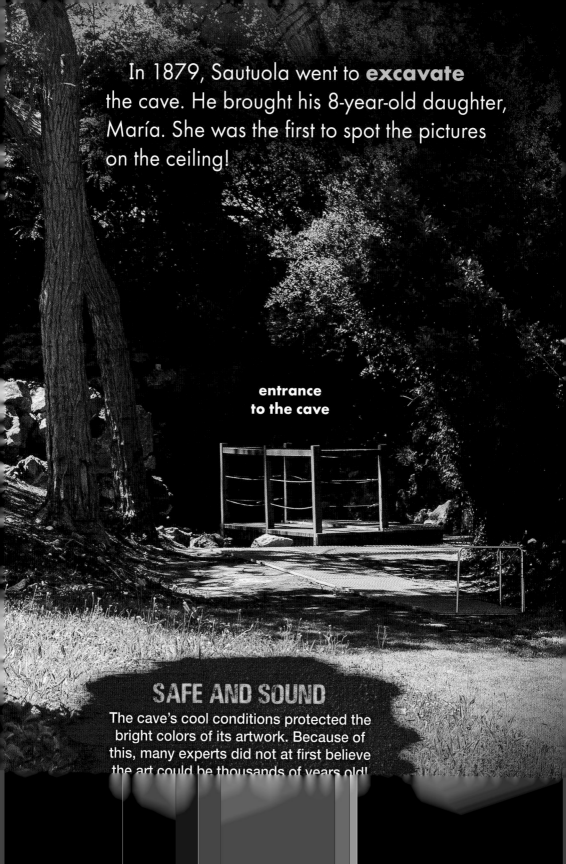

In 1879, Sautuola went to **excavate** the cave. He brought his 8-year-old daughter, María. She was the first to spot the pictures on the ceiling!

entrance
to the cave

SAFE AND SOUND

The cave's cool conditions protected the bright colors of its artwork. Because of this, many experts did not at first believe the art could be thousands of years old!

María had discovered the Polychrome Chamber. The chamber was named for the many colors painted on its ceiling. Deer, horses, and bison crowded part of its ceiling. They were painted black, red, violet, and yellow.

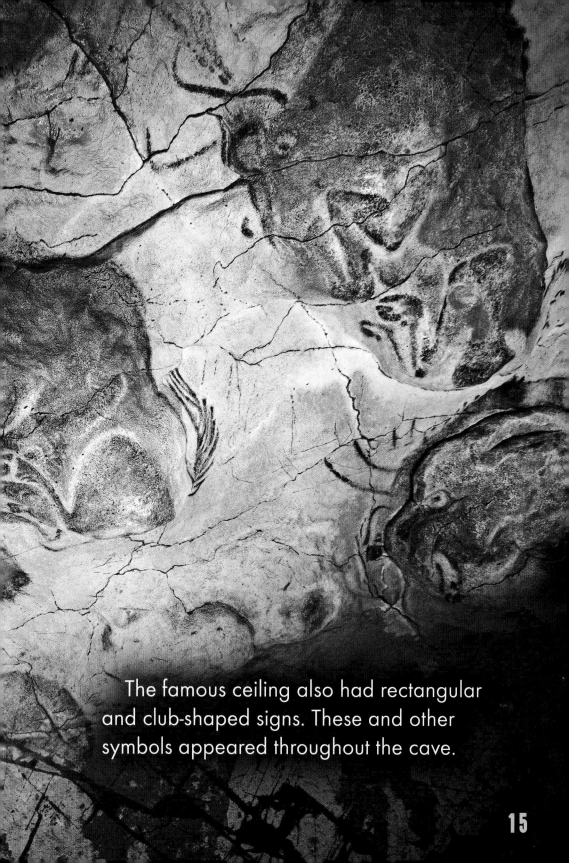

The famous ceiling also had rectangular and club-shaped signs. These and other symbols appeared throughout the cave.

Deep in the cave were rocks that naturally looked like faces. These are now known as masks. Artists used charcoal or paint to add eyes and hair.

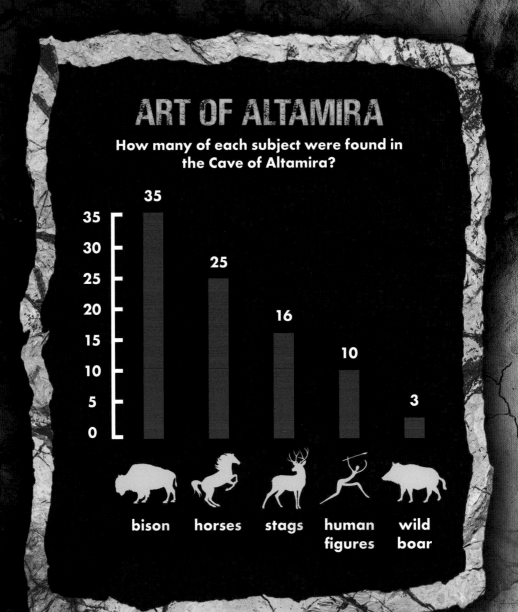

ART OF ALTAMIRA

How many of each subject were found in the Cave of Altamira?

bison	35
horses	25
stags	16
human figures	10
wild boar	3

LARGEST FIGURE

The biggest figure in the cave is a doe.
It is about 8.2 feet (2.5 meters) long.
The picture is as large as a real doe!

Altamira's discovery changed common ideas about Paleolithic humans. It showed that prehistoric humans could create beautiful art!

PRESERVING ALTAMIRA

Altamira has taught scientists a lot about Paleolithic people. Art and other items found there tell stories about prehistoric life.

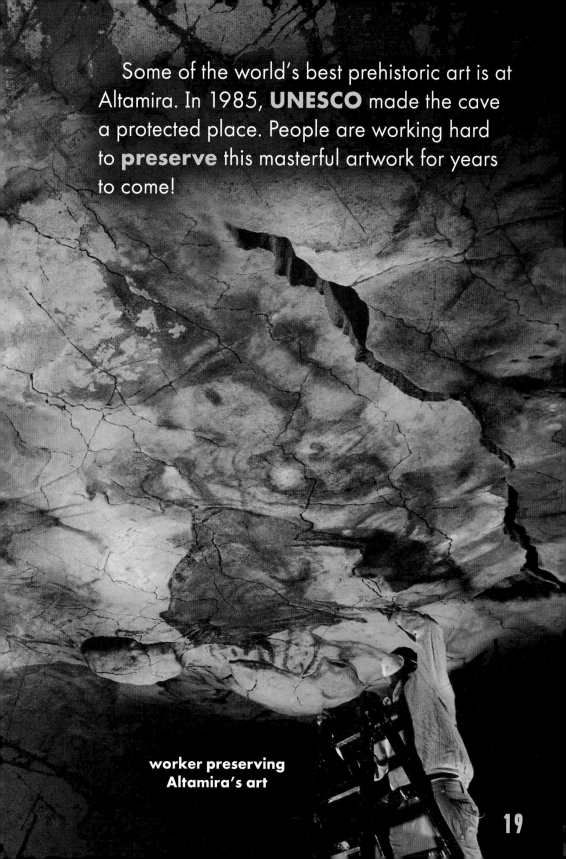

Some of the world's best prehistoric art is at Altamira. In 1985, **UNESCO** made the cave a protected place. People are working hard to **preserve** this masterful artwork for years to come!

**worker preserving
Altamira's art**

PRESERVED IN PAINT

Discovery: Cave of Altamira was painted over a period of 20,000 years

Date of Discovery: 2008

Process:

1. Tiny samples from the top layers of the cave art taken by researchers
2. Samples are tested for levels of the elements thorium and uranium
3. Samples are given an age by researchers based on the levels

What It Means:

- Altamira not painted all at once
- Altamira's oldest paintings more than 20,000 years old
- Humans did not live in cave, just visited it

In 2002, the cave closed to the public. Harmful **mold** grew inside the cave and damaged the art. Today, just a few visitors can go inside each week.

Tourists can still visit the nearby museum and cave replica. The cave's copy allows visitors to imagine the lives of early humans. It lets them experience the wonder of this prehistoric treasure!

21

GLOSSARY

collapsed—fell down or caved in

engravings—carvings

estimate—to make a guess

excavate—to dig up

Ice Age—a long period when much of Earth is covered in glaciers; the last Ice Age ended around 11,700 years ago.

mold—a growth that develops in warm, moist areas

nobleman—a man who was born into a wealthy or noble family

Paleolithic—related to an early period of human history when the first tools were made of stone; the Paleolithic period ended around 11,700 years ago.

prehistoric—related to a time in history before there were written records

preserve—to protect

replica—an exact copy

symbols—images, words, or other signs that represent something else

tourists—people who travel to visit another place

UNESCO—a worldwide organization that works to protect important pieces of culture; UNESCO stands for United Nations Educational, Scientific, and Cultural Organization.

TO LEARN MORE

AT THE LIBRARY

Huey, Lois Miner. *Children of the Past: Archaeology and the Lives of Kids*. Minneapolis, Minn.: Millbrook Press, 2017.

Lock, Deborah. *Secrets of the Cave*. New York, N.Y.: DK Publishing, 2015.

Medina, Nico. *What Was the Ice Age?* New York, N.Y.: Penguin Workshop, 2017.

ON THE WEB

FACTSURFER

Factsurfer.com gives you a safe, fun way to find more information.

1. Go to www.factsurfer.com.

2. Enter "Cave of Altamira" into the search box and click 🔍.

3. Select your book cover to see a list of related web sites.

INDEX